ALFRED'S BASIC GUITAR POP SONGS 1 & 2

Contents

Title	Page	Listening Track	Play-Along Track
Telstar	2	2	3
As Tears Go By	3	4	5
Peaceful Easy Feeling	4	6	7
Wildwood Flower	6	8	9
Take It Easy	8	10	11
Do You Want to Know a Secret	10	12	13
Boulevard of Broken Dreams	14	14	15
Mr. Bojangles	20	16	17
Smooth	24	18	19
Sunshine of Your Love	30	20	21
Layla (Unplugged)	36	22	23

About the CD: There are two audio tracks for each song: a full "listening" version for demonstration, and a special "play-along" version that allows you to remove the guitar part from the mix so you can play along with just the accompaniment. To use the play-along track, turn the balance all the way to the right to drop out the guitar and hear only the accompaniment. For duets, turn the balance all the way left to drop out Guitar 2 and all the way right to drop out Guitar 1.

About the MP3 files: The MP3 files are accompaniment-only tracks for easy practicing without the need for a balance control. To copy the files to your computer, place the CD in your computer's CD-ROM drive. In Windows, double click on "My Computer," then right-click on the CD icon labeled "MP3 FILES" and select "Explore" to view the files and copy them to your hard drive. For Mac, double-click the CD icon on your desktop labeled "MP3 FILES" to view the files and copy them to your hard drive.

Guitars, bass, and mandolin: Dan Warner
Drums: Lee Levin
Keyboards: Doug Emory

Track 1

Use track 1 on the CD to tune your guitar.

ISBN-10: 0-7390-4884-8 (Book and CD)
ISBN-13: 978-0-7390-4884-9 (Book and CD)

Cover photo courtesy of Daisy Rock Guitars

Alfred Publishing Co., Inc.
16320 Roscoe Blvd., Suite 100
P.O. Box 10003
Van Nuys, CA 91410-0003
alfred.com

*Use after page 20
of Alfred's Basic Guitar Method, Book 1.*

Tip: The repeat sign at measure 16 takes you back to the beginning of the song.
The second time through the song, play through the repeat and end on the last measure.

Telstar

By JOE MEEK

Moderately

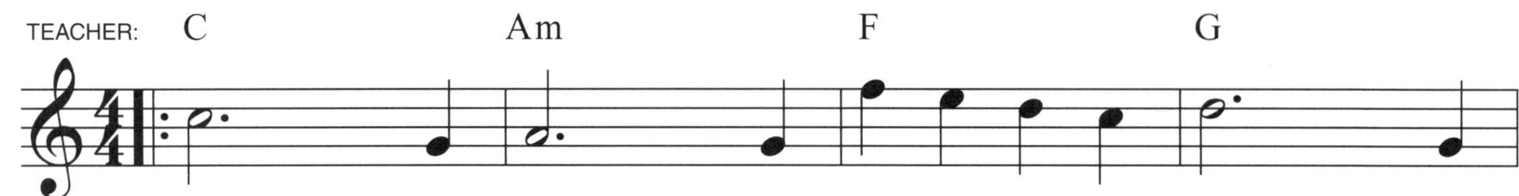

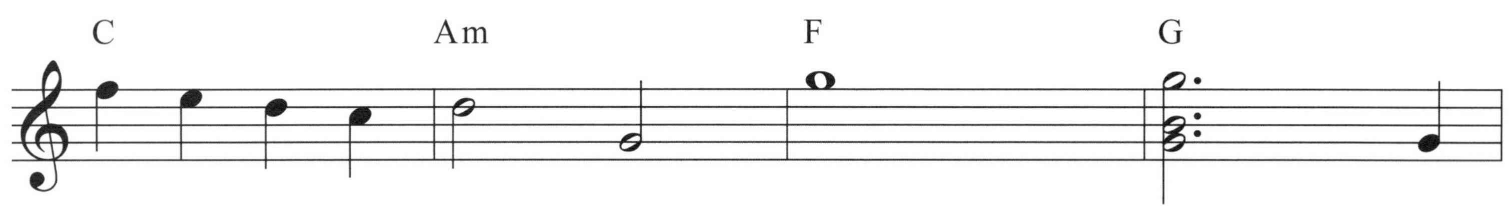

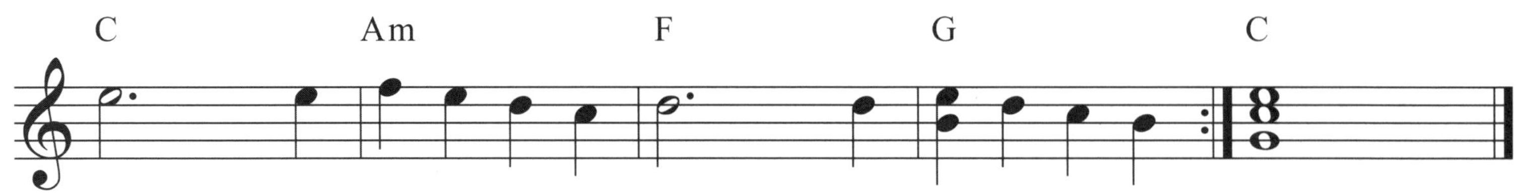

*Use after page 22
of Alfred's Basic Guitar Method, Book 1.*

Tip: Measures 15 and 16 use a series of two-note chords. Just focus
on the top notes: D–C–B–C–D. The bottom note of each chord is the open G string.

As Tears Go By

Words and Music by
MICK JAGGER, KEITH RICHARDS
and ANDREW LOOG OLDHAM

Moderately slow

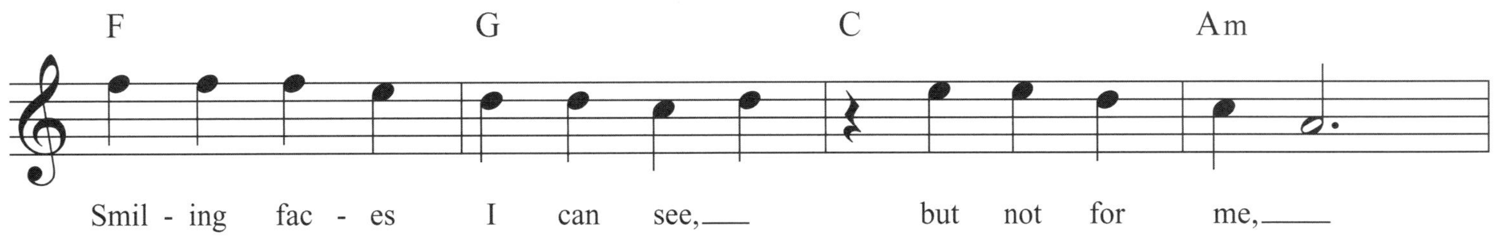

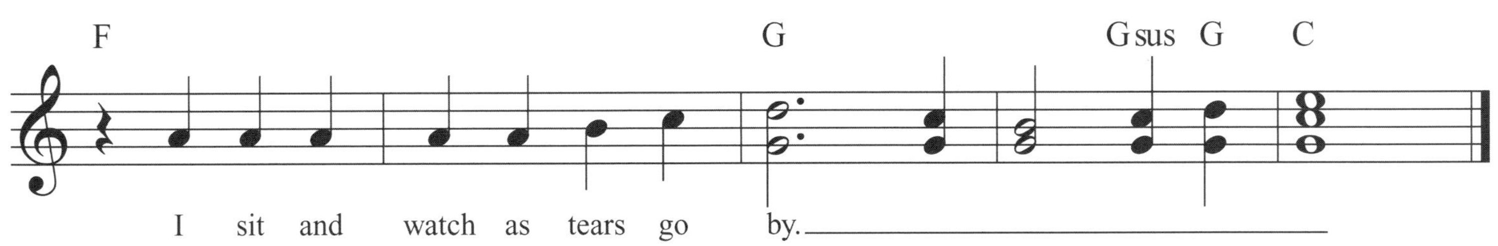

*Use after page 28
of Alfred's Basic Guitar Method, Book 1.*

Tip: In measures 1 through 4, hold the 1st-string G for the full four measures.
The 2nd, 3rd, and 4th strings are open in measures 1 and 3. Add your 1st finger
to the 2nd-string C for measures 2 and 4.

Peaceful Easy Feeling

Tracks 6-7

Words and Music by
JACK TEMPCHIN

Chorus:

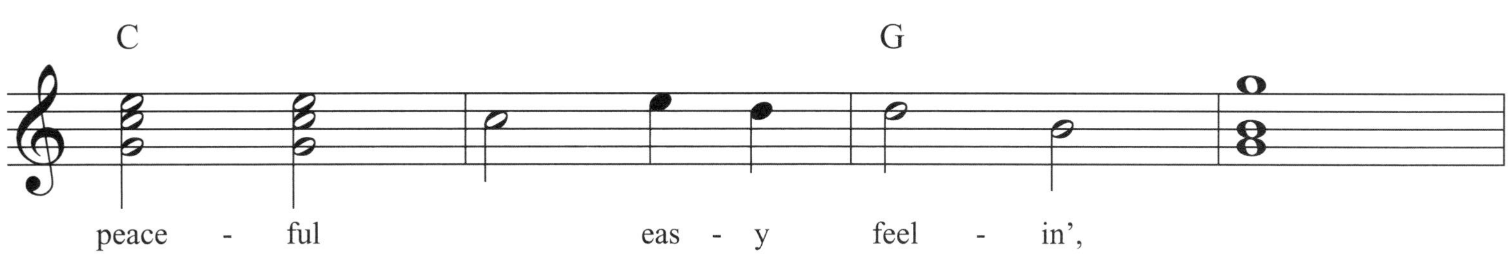

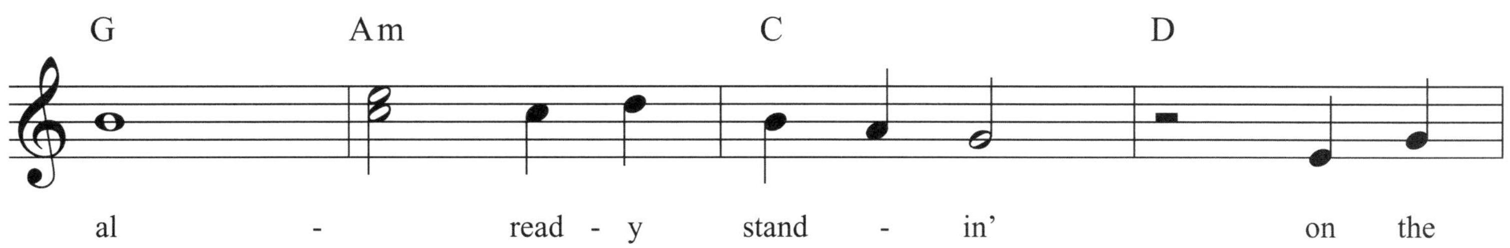

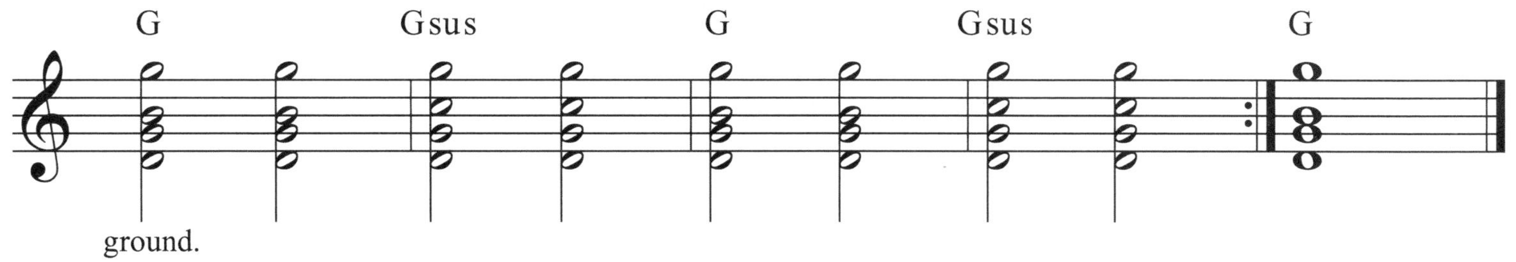

Additional Lyrics

Verse 2:
And I found out a long time ago
What a woman can do to your soul.
Ah, but she can take you any way,
You don't already know.
(To Chorus:)

Verse 3:
I get this feelin' I may know you
As a lover and a friend.
But this voice keeps whispering in my other ear,
Tells me I may never see you again.
(To Chorus:)

Tip: This is a classic example of bass-chord style, which was made famous by "Mother" Maybelle Carter. An authentic traditional version is featured in the Johnny Cash biographical film *I Walk the Line*.

Wildwood Flower

(I'll Twine 'Mid the Ringlets)

Words and Music by
MAUDE IRVING and J.D. WEBSTER

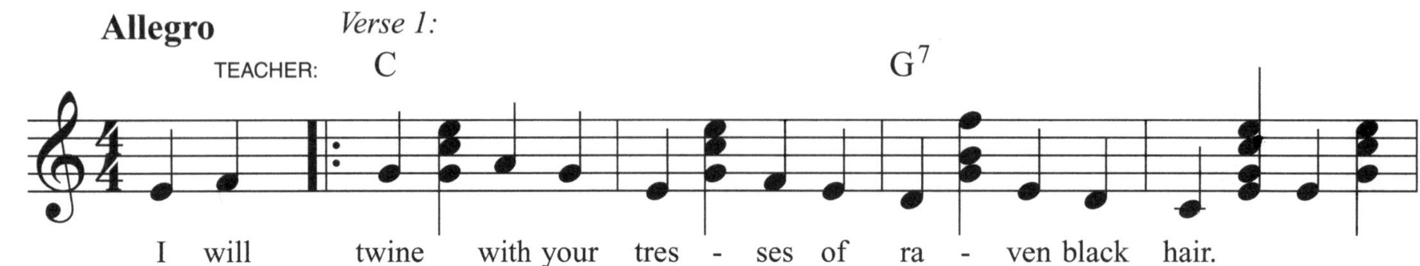

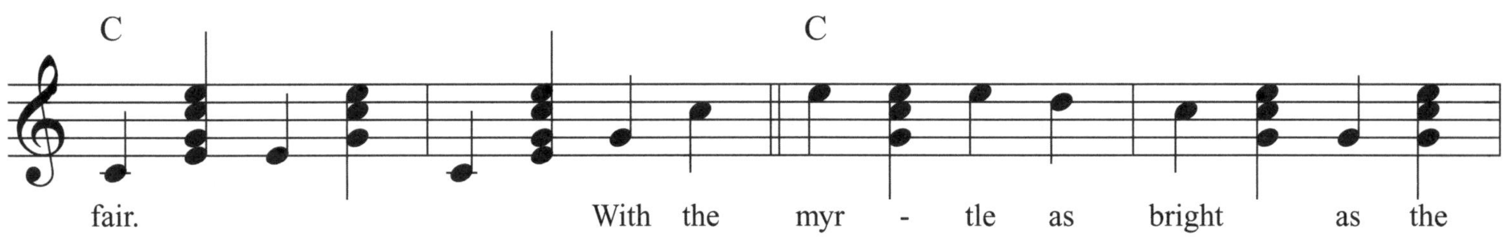

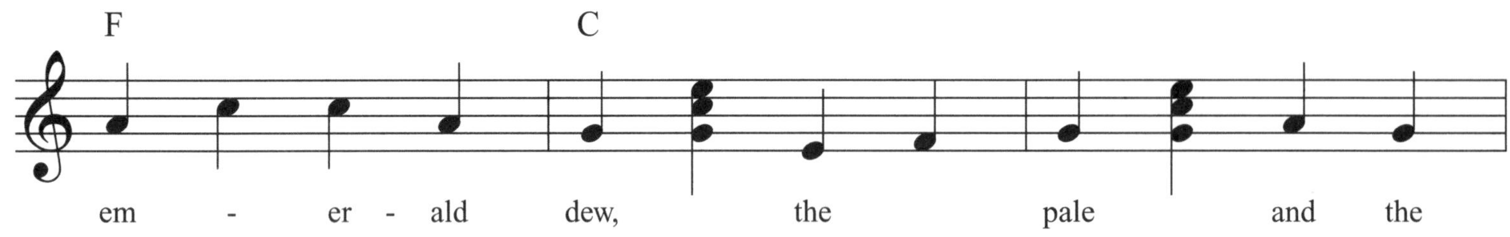

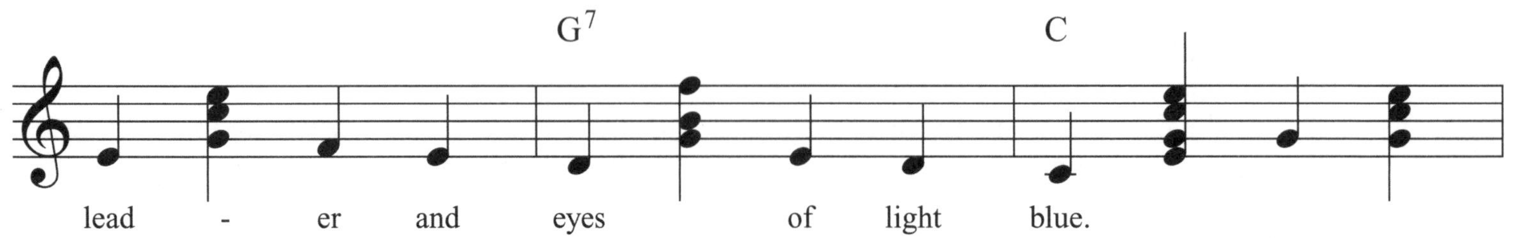

Verse 2:

C
G7
Oh I'll dance, I will sing and my laugh shall be

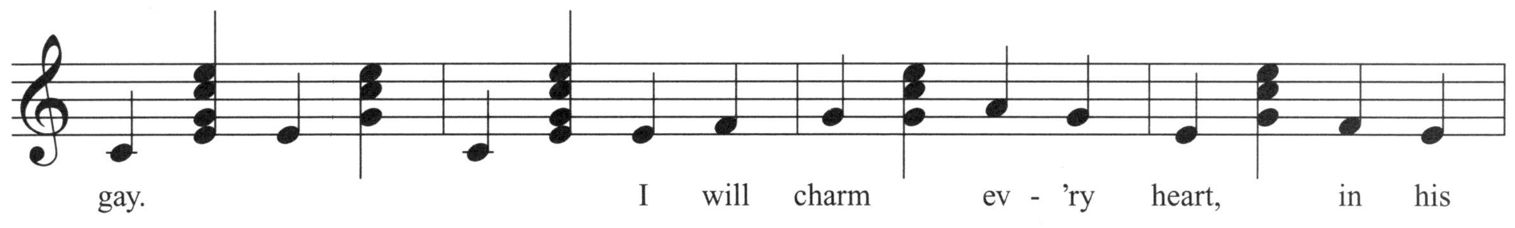
gay. I will charm ev - 'ry heart, in his

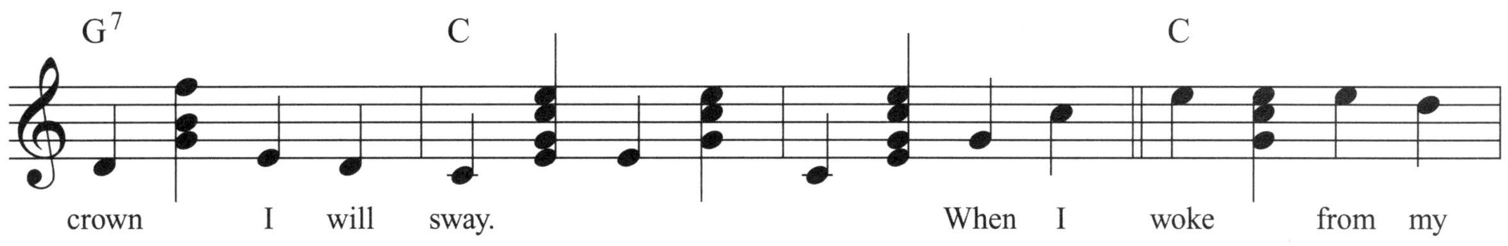
G7
C
C
crown I will sway. When I woke from my

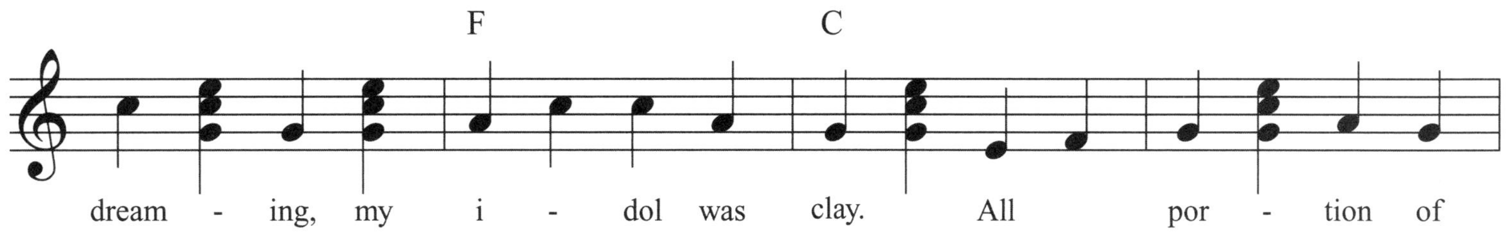
F
C
dream - ing, my i - dol was clay. All por - tion of

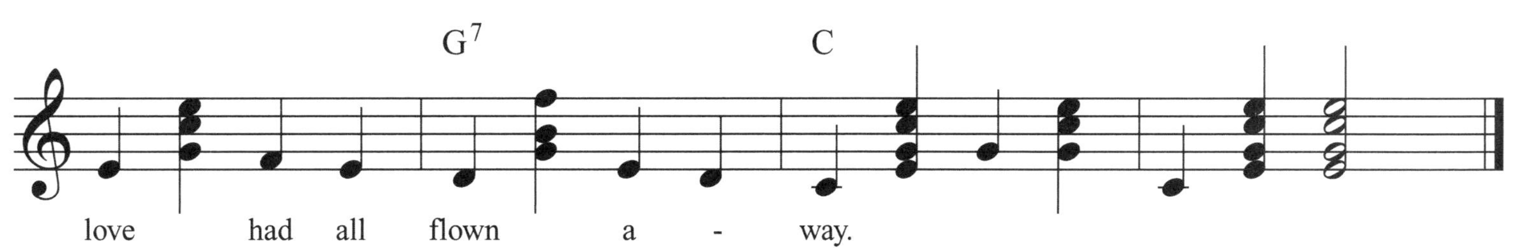
G7
C
love had all flown a - way.

Use after page 46
of Alfred's Basic Guitar Method, Book 1.

Tip: Use strict alternate picking (down-up) to play the eighth-note passages.

Take It Easy 

Words and Music by
JACKSON BROWNE and GLENN FREY

Moderately

Verse:

TEACHER: G

D   C   G

D   C   G

Chorus:
Em   C   G

Am   C   Em

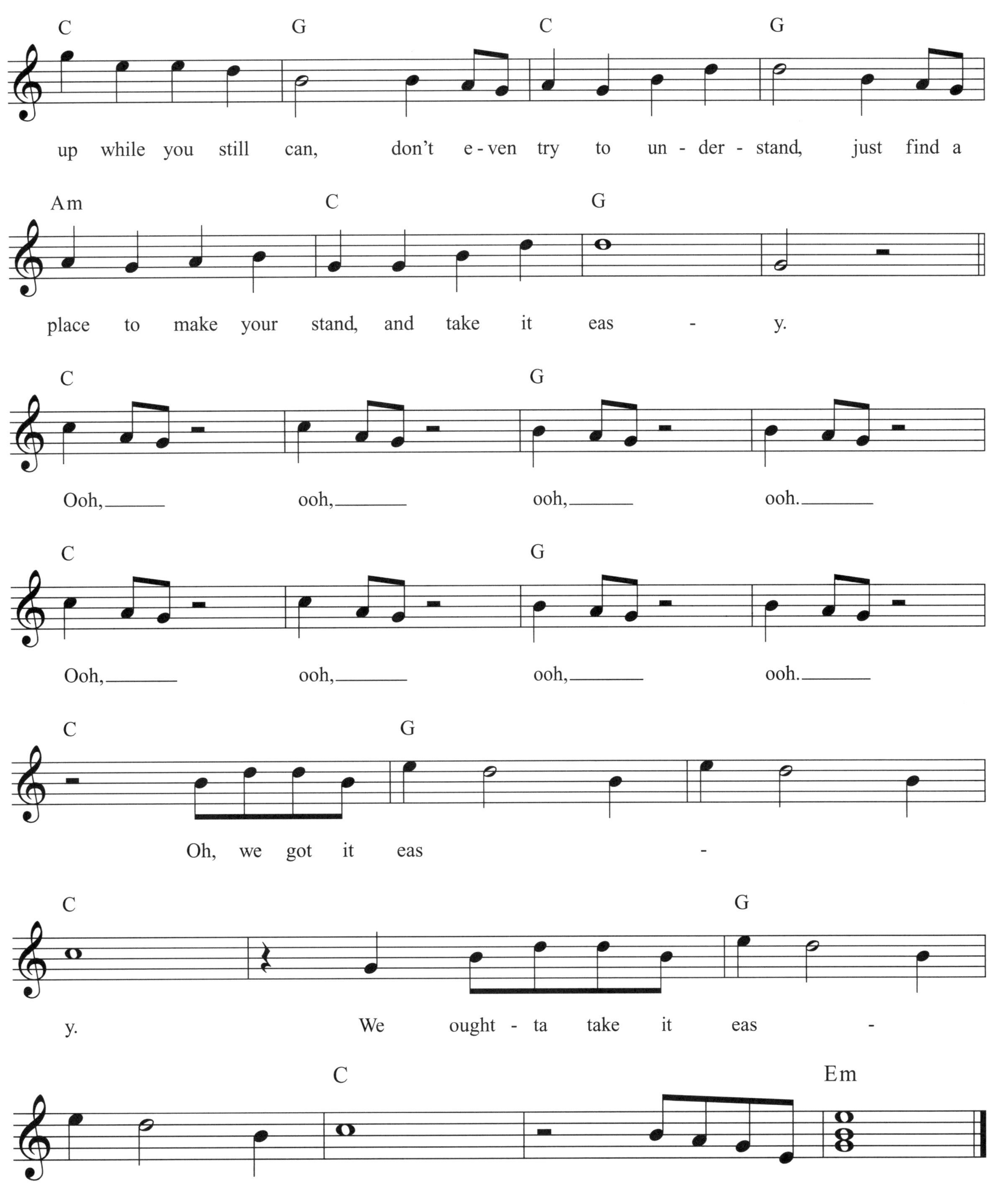
C
G
C
G
up while you still can, don't e-ven try to un-der-stand, just find a
Am
C
G
place to make your stand, and take it eas - y.
C
G
Ooh, ooh, ooh, ooh.
C
G
Ooh, ooh, ooh, ooh.
C
G
Oh, we got it eas -
C
G
y. We ought-ta take it eas -
C
Em
y.

Use after page 58
of Alfred's Basic Guitar Method, Book 1.

Tip: In this duet, Guitar 1 plays the melody and uses eighth notes, rests, and chromatic notes.
Guitar 2 uses many simple three-note chords and is ideal for your teacher to play.
If you want to challenge yourself now and play Guitar 2, use the chord diagrams above
the staff to learn the fingerings for those chords. It may be challenging to play the Guitar 2
part now, but you can always come back and play it later.

Do You Want to Know a Secret
(duet)

Words and Music by
JOHN LENNON and PAUL McCARTNEY

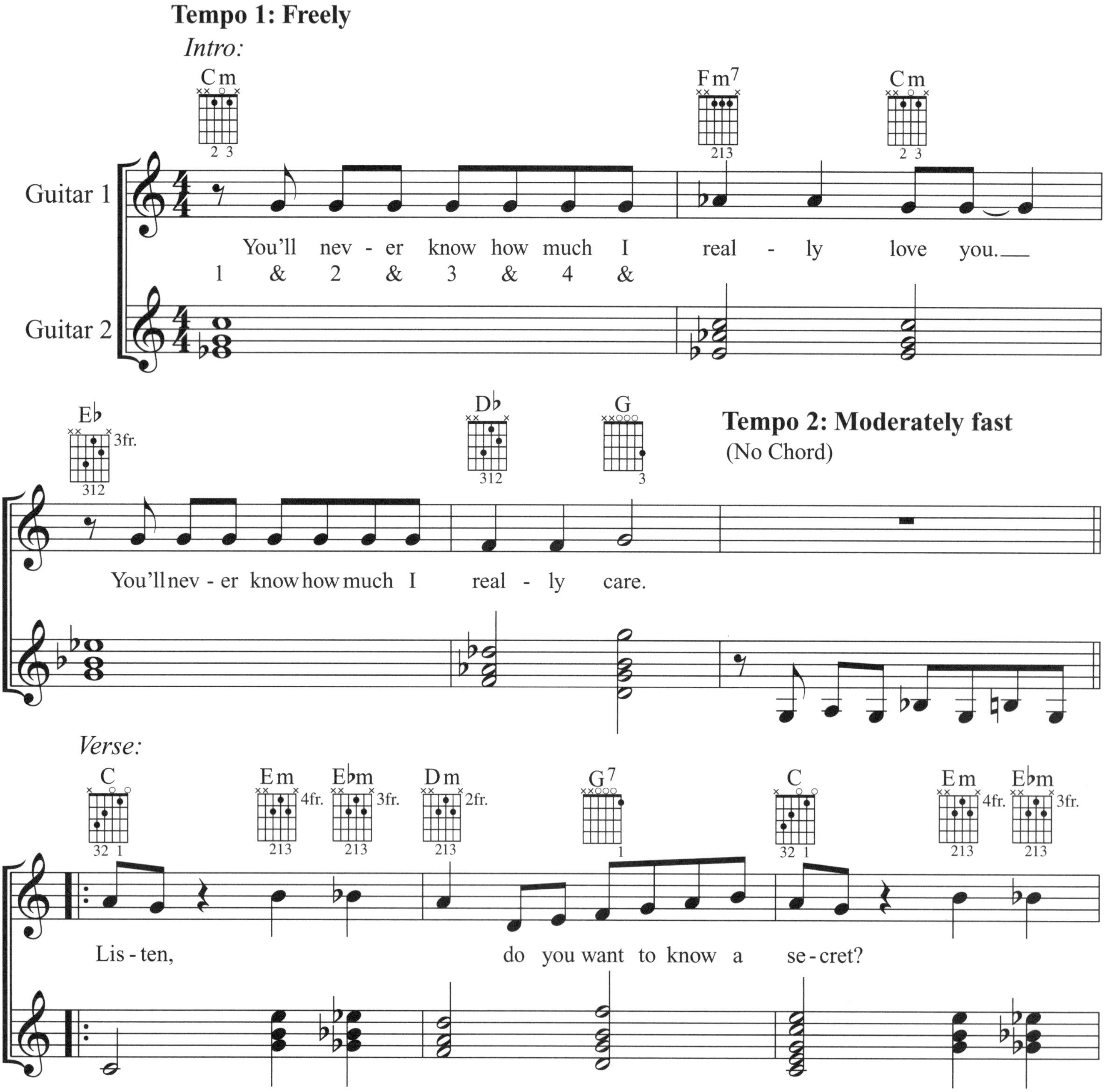

Do you prom-ise not to tell? Woah.
Clos - er, let me whis-per in your ear.
Say the words you long to hear. I'm in love with
you, ooh.

Bridge:
F Dm Am Gm F Dm
I've known a se-cret for a week or two.___ No-bod-y knows;
1 & 2 & 3 4
Am Gm Dm G
just we two.___
Verse:
C Em Ebm Dm G7 C Em Ebm
Lis-ten, do you want to know a se-cret?
Dm G7 C Em Ebm Dm Db
Do you prom-ise not to tell? Woah.___

C
Em
E♭m
Dm
G7
C
Em
E♭m
Clos - er,
let me whis-per in your ear.
Dm
G7
F
G
Say the words you long to hear.
I'm in love with
Am
Dm
G7
Am
you,
ooh.
Ooh.
Dm
G7
Am
Dm
G7
A
rit.
Ooh.
rit.

*Use after page 60
of Alfred's Basic Guitar Method, Book 1.*

Tip: Guitar 2 of this arrangement is based on the actual part played by Green Day.
It consists of two-note chords played on the lower strings. If you want to challenge
yourself now and play Guitar 2, use the chord grids above the staff to find the fingerings.

Boulevard of Broken Dreams
(duet)

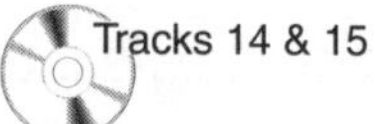

Words by BILLIE JOE
Music by GREEN DAY

Moderately fast

Guitar 1

Guitar 2

E5 G D5 A5

Verses 1 & 2:

E5 G D5 A5

1. I walk a lone - ly road, the on - ly one that I have ev - er
2. I'm walk - in' down the line that di - vides me some - where in my

E5   G   D5   A5
known. Don't know where it goes, but it's home to me I walk a-
mind. On the bor-der-line of the edge and where I walk a-
E5   G   D5   A5
lone.
lone.
E5   G   D5   A5
I walk this emp-ty street on the bou-le-vard of bro-ken
Read be-tween the lines, of what's messed up and ev-'ry-thing's al-
E5   G   D5   A5
dreams, where the cit-y sleeps and I'm the on-ly one, I walk a-
right. Check my vi-tal signs and know I'm still a-live, I walk a-

E5
G
D5
A5
lone.
lone.
I walk a - lone, I walk a -
E5
G
D5
A5
lone.
I walk a - lone, I walk a...
Chorus:
C
G
D
Em
My shad - ow's the on - ly one that walks be - side me.
C
G
D
Em
My shal - low heart's the on - ly thing that's beat - ing.

C   G   D   Em
Some - times__ I   wish some - one out there will find me.
C   G   B5   E5   G
'Til then__ I   walk a - lone.   Ah.__   Ah.__
D5   A5   E5   G
Ah.__   Ah.__   Ah.__   Ah.__   I walk a-lone, I walk a...
Instrumental Solo:
C   G   D   Em   C   G

D
Em
C
G
D
Em
C
G
B5   2fr.
Verse 3:
E5
G
D5
A5
I walk this emp - ty street on the bou - le - vard of bro - ken
E5
G
D5
A5
dreams, where the cit - y sleeps and I'm the on - ly one I walk a...

Chorus:
C   G   D   Em   C   G
My shad-ow's the on-ly one that walks be-side me.   My shal-low
D   Em   C   G   D   Em
heart's the on-ly thing that's beat-ing.   Some-times_ I wish some-one out there will find me.
C   G   B5
'Til then_ I walk a-lone._
Outro:
N.C. (no chord)
(Em)   (C)   (D)   (A)   (G)   (B)   N.C.
Play 4 times

Tip: In this duet, Guitar 1 has the melody and Guitar 2 plays the accompaniment. This song is usually played with a *swing* feel, meaning the eighth-note pairs are played long-short. Listen to the recording, and imitate the rhythm you hear. You may want to challenge yourself and play the accompaniment part. In the Intro, the accompaniment guitar holds the chords indicated above the staff and picks out the notes, using down-strokes throughout. There are a few new chords, such as A7, so use the chord grids and music notation to learn them.

Mr. Bojangles
(duet)

Tracks 16

Words and Music by
JERRY JEFF WALKER

G
G/F#
G/E
G/D
Sil - ver hair, and rag - ged shirt and bag - gy pants,_______
C
D
the old___ soft___ shoe.___
C
Bm7
B7
He jumped so_____ high.
He jumped so high_
Em
Em/D
A7
___ and then he light - ly touched_ down.

D
1.
2.3.
1. I
2. He
Chorus:
Em9
D
Mis - ter Bo - jan - gles,
Em9
D
Mis - ter Bo - jan - gles,
Em9
D
Mis - ter Bo - jan - gles,

Verse 2:
I met him in a cell in New Orleans, I was
down ind out.
He looked to me to be the eyes of age
as he spoke right out.
He talked of life, he talked of life.
He laughed, he clicked his heels and stepped.
(To Chorus:)

Verse 3:
He said, " I danced now at every chance in honky tonks
For drinks and tips.
But most the time I spend behind these county bars
'Cause I drinks a bit."
He shook his head.
And as he shook his head,
I heard someone ask him, "Please, please,"…
(To Chorus:)

Use after page 20
of Alfred's Basic Guitar Method, Book 2.

Tip: Learn both parts of this duet. This song uses lots of syncopation, so count carefully.
There are many notated chords, so refer to the chord grids above the staff for fingerings.

Smooth 
(duet)

Words and Music by
ITAAL SHUR and ROB THOMAS

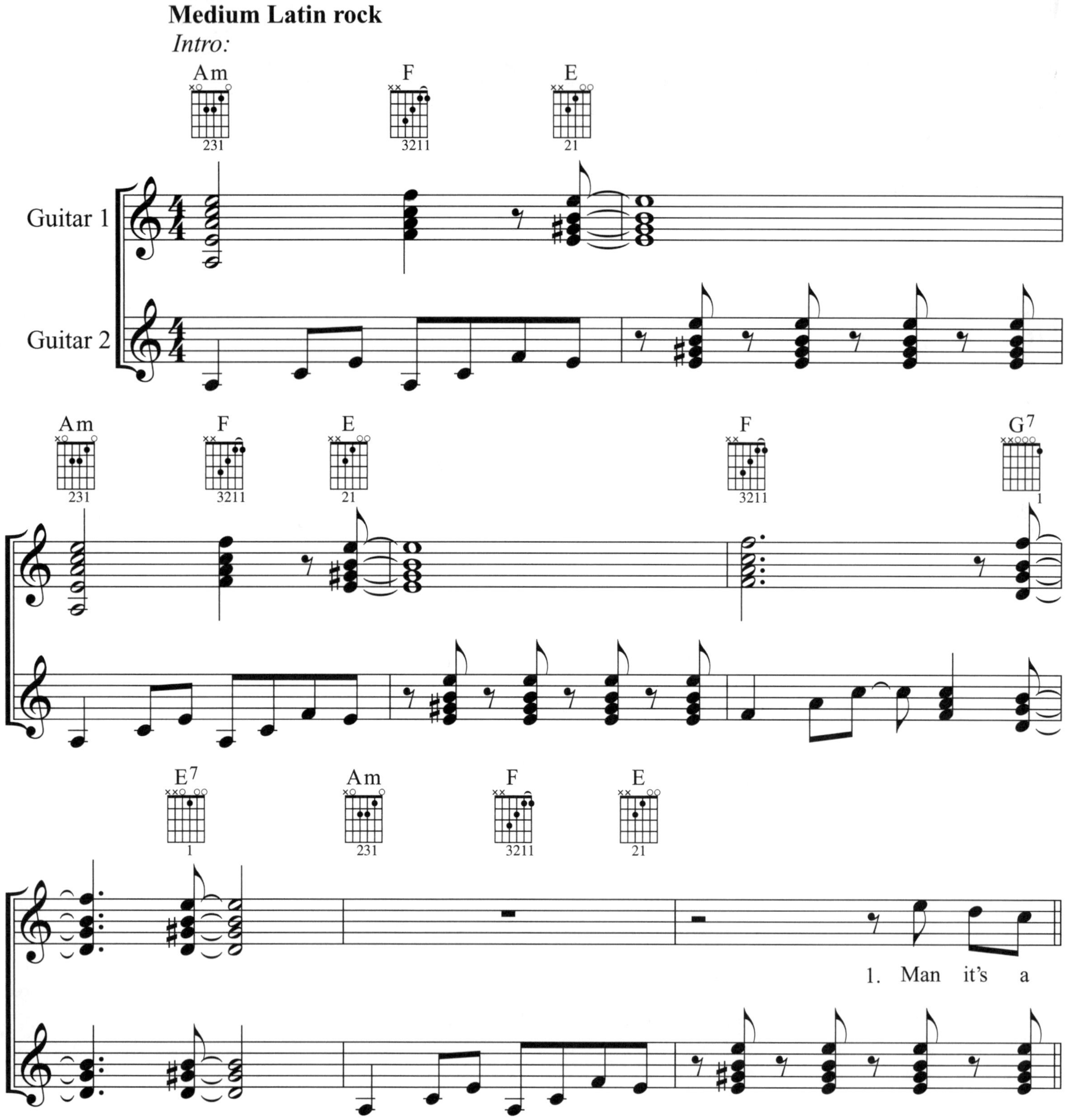

Verse:

Am F E Am F E
231 3211 21 231 3211 21
hot one,
(2.) one thing
like sev - en inch - es from the mid-day sun.
if you would leave it be a cry-in' shame.

F G7
3211 1
Well, I hear your whis - per and the words melt ev - 'ry
In ev - 'ry breath and ev - 'ry word I hear your

E7 Am F E
1 231 3211 21
one. But you stay so cool.
name call - ing me out.
My Mu - ñe -
Well, out from the

Am F E Am F E
231 3211 21 231 3211 21
qui - ta,
bar - rio
my Span - ish Har - lem Mo - na Li - sa.
you hear my rhy - thm on your ra - di - o.

F
G7
You're my rea - son for rea - son;
You feel the turn - ing of the world so soft and
E7
Am
F
E
the step in my groove.
slow, turn - ing you 'round.
And if you said,
Am
F
E
Am
F
E
"This life ain't good e - nough," I would give my world to
Am
F
E
lift you up. I could change my life to bet - ter suit your mood.

Dm7
G7
"'Cause you're so
F#7sus
B7sus
E7(#9)
smooth.
Oh, and it's
Chorus:
Am
F
E
just like the o - cean under the moon.__ It's the
Am
F
E
same as the e - mo - tion that I get from you.__ You

Am
F
E
got the kind of lov - ing that can be so smooth._
Dm7
E7
1.
Am
F
E
Give me your heart,_ make it real or else for - get a - bout it.
Am
F
E
2. Well, I'll tell you
2.
Instrumental:
Am
F
E
Am
F
E

Am
231
F
3211
E
21
Am
231
F
3211
E
21
Dm7
211
G7
1
Dm7
211
E7
1
Am
231

Tip: Learn both parts of this duet. This song uses lots of syncopation, so count carefully. There are some new chords, like D5 and C5. Refer to the chord grids for fingerings.

Sunshine of Your Love
(duet)

Tracks 20

Words and Music by
JACK BRUCE, PETE BROWN
and ERIC CLAPTON

D5
C5
D5
lights close their tired____ eyes.____________ I'll
light shin - ing through__ on you.____________ Yes, I'm

D5
C5
D5
soon be with you,___ my__ love,____________ to
with you, my love.___ It's the

D5
C5
D5
give you my dawn__ sur - prise.____________ I'll
morn - ing and just__ we__ two.____________ I'll

G5
F5
G5
be with you, dar - ling, soon.____________ I'll
stay with you, dar - ling, now.____________ I'll

G5   F5   G5
5fr.   3fr.   5fr.
13   13   13
soon   be   with   you____   when   the   stars____   start____   fall - ing.
stay   with   you   till____   my   seas____   are____   dried____   up.
D5   C5   D5
5fr.   3fr.   5fr.
13   13   13
D5   C5   D5
5fr.   3fr.   5fr.
13   13   13
To Coda
Chorus:
A5   C   G   A5
1   32 1   21 3   1
I've__   been   wait - ing   so__   long   to__   be   where__

C
G
A5
C
G
I'm go - ing in the sun - shine of your
A5
1.
D5 C5 D5
love.
2.
D5 C5 D5
2. I'm
D5 C5 D5
D.S. % al Coda
3. I'm

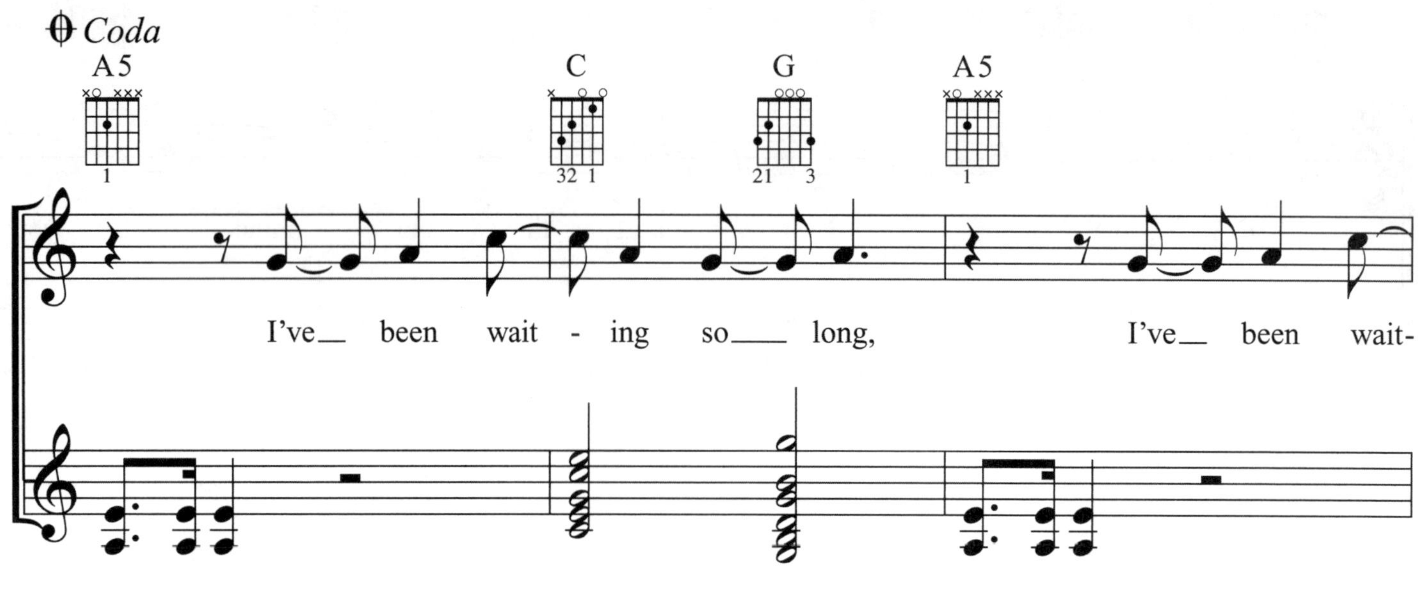
Coda
A5   C   G   A5
I've__ been wait - ing so__ long,   I've__ been wait-

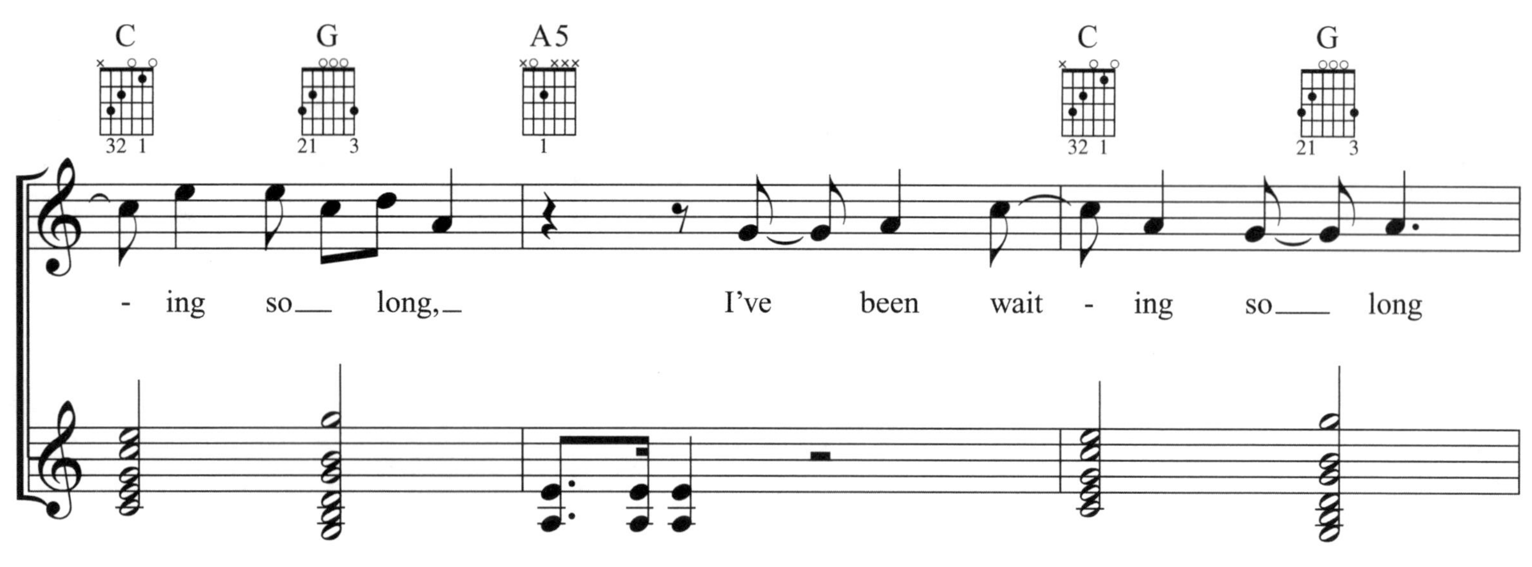
C   G   A5   C   G
- ing so__ long,__   I've been wait - ing so__ long

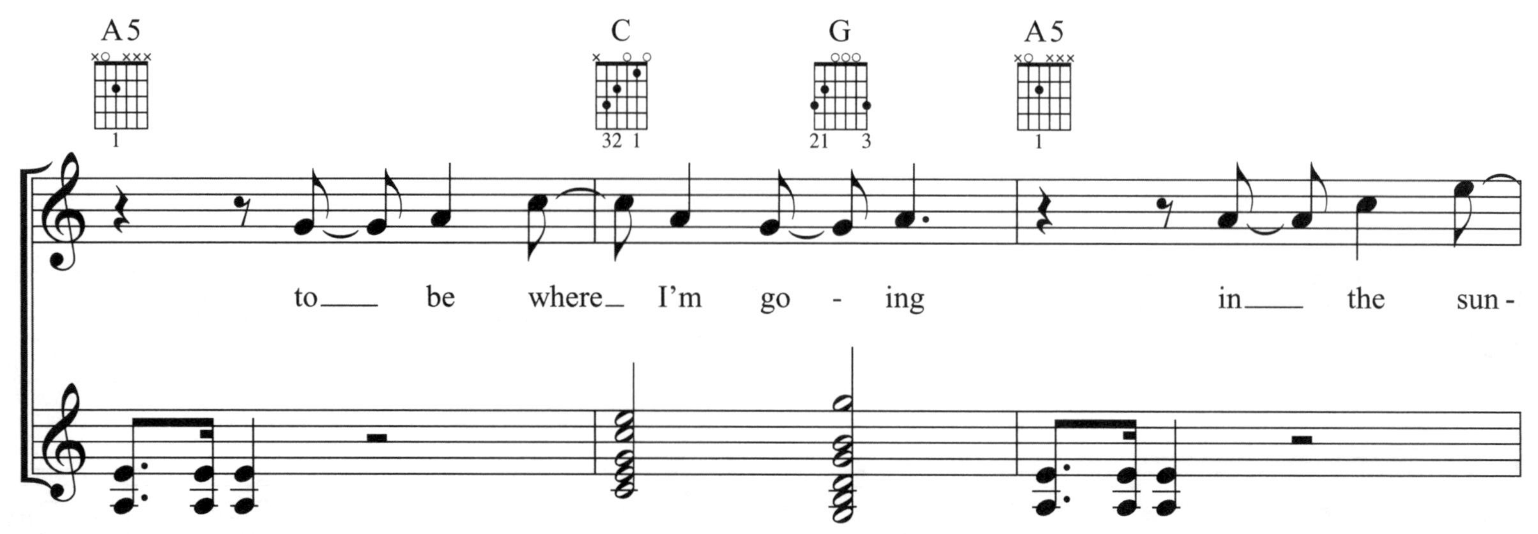
A5   C   G   A5
to__ be where__ I'm go - ing   in__ the sun-

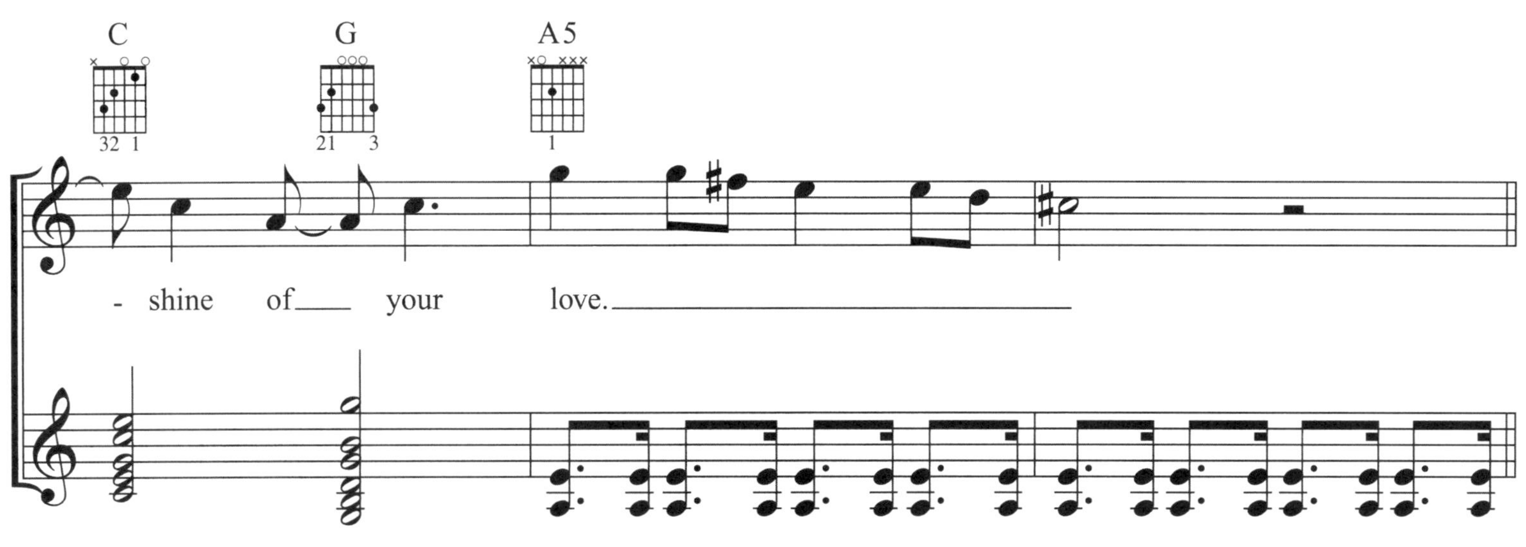

C
G
A5
- shine   of___   your   love._______________________________

D5
C5   D5

D5
C5   D5
D5   C5   D5

Use after page 38
of Alfred's Basic Guitar Method, Book 2.

Tip: Guitar 1 has the guitar solos and the melody. Guitar 2 plays the rhythm guitar part.
This is a very syncopated song, but if you listen carefully to the recording and make sure
you have all the chord fingerings firmly "under your fingers," you'll be able to play this
without too much trouble.

Layla (Unplugged)
(duet)

Tracks 22

Words and Music by
ERIC CLAPTON and JIM GORDON

Verse:
C#m G# C#m C D
1. What'll you do when you get lone - ly?___ No-one wait-ing by your
2. Tried to give you con - so - la - tion,___ your old man has let you
3. Make the best of the sit - u - a - tion be - fore I fi-n'lly go in -

E E7 F#m B7 E A
side. You been run - nin',___ hid - ing much too long,_____
down. Like a fool I_____ fell in love with you,_____
sane. Please don't say we'll nev - er find a way_____

F#m B7 E A5 D5
you know it's just your fool - ish pride. }
you turned my whole world up - side down. } Lay - la,___
and tell me all my love's in vain. }

Chorus:
Bb5 C D5 Bb5 C
___ you got me on my knees. Lay - la,___ I

D5
Bb5
C
D5
beg you, dar-lin', please. Lay - la,_____ dar-lin', won't you ease my wor-ried

Bb5
C
1.2.
3.
N.C.
D5
mind? Lay -

Bb5
C
D5
Bb5
C
la, you got me on my knees. Lay - la,_____ I

To Coda
D5
Bb5
C
beg you, dar - lin', please.   Lay - la,______
D.S. al Coda
D5
Bb5
C
D5
dar - lin', won't you ease my wor-ried mind?   Lay -
Coda
Dm
dar - lin', won't you ease my wor - ried mind?
rit. (slow down)

CHORD ACCOMPANIMENT GUIDE

Key	The **Three Principal Chords**			The **Relative Minor Chords**			Alternate Chords					
	I	**IV**	**V7**	**i**	**iv**	**V7**						
A♭	A♭	D♭	E♭7	Fm	B♭m	C7	A♭6	A♭dim.	A♭aug.	D♭6	Fm6	B♭m6
A	A	D	E7	F#m	Bm	C#7	A6	Adim.	Aaug.	D6	F#m6	Bm6
B♭	B♭	E♭	F7	Gm	Cm	D7	B♭6	B♭dim.	B♭aug.	E♭6	Gm6	Cm6
B	B	E	F#7	A♭m	D♭m	E♭7	B6	Bdim.	Baug.	E6	G#m6	C#m6
C	C	F	G7	Am	Dm	E7	C6	Cdim.	Caug.	F6	Am6	Dm6
D♭	D♭	G♭	A♭7	B♭m	E♭m	F7	D♭6	D♭dim.	D♭aug.	G♭6	B♭m6	E♭m6
D	D	G	A7	Bm	Em	F#7	D6	Ddim.	Daug.	G6	Bm6	Em6
E♭	E♭	A♭	B♭7	Cm	Fm	G7	E♭6	E♭dim.	E♭aug.	A♭6	Cm6	Fm6
E	E	A	B7	C#m	F#m	G#7	E6	Edim.	Eaug.	A6	C#m6	F#m6
F	F	B♭	C7	Dm	Gm	A7	F6	Fdim.	Faug.	B♭6	Dm6	Gm6
F#	F#	B	C#7	E♭m	A♭m	B♭7	F#6	F#dim.	F#aug.	B6	D#m6	G#m6
G	G	C	D7	Em	Am	B7	G6	Gdim.	Gaug.	C6	Em6	Am6